TABLE OF CONTENTS

Unless otherwise indicated, all Scripture quotations are taken from the King James Version of the Bible.

Seeds Of Wisdom On Productivity
ISBN 1-56394-215-1
Copyright © 2002 by *MIKE MURDOCK*
All publishing rights belong exclusively to Wisdom International
Published by The Wisdom Center
P. O. Box 99 · Denton, Texas 76202 · 1-888-WISDOM-1 (1-888-947-3661)
Website: www.thewisdomcenter.cc

When Your Heart
Decides The Destination...
Your Mind Will Design
The Map To Reach It.

-MIKE MURDOCK

❧ 1 ❧

DECIDE WHAT YOU WANT MOST.

Your Goals Will Change Throughout Your Life. Someday, you will look back at this very moment and be amazed at the goals you presently have. Things so vital to you at 20 years of age will become unimportant to you at 30.

When I was beginning my ministry, I wanted very much to minister in many different states and cities. Times have changed. Needs have changed. My personal goals have changed. Today, staying home excites me. Knowing that my books are being read in many places is far more satisfying to me than traveling. The greatest goal of my life today is staying in my Secret Place of prayer and writing what the Holy Spirit teaches me through His Word and daily experiences.

These kinds of good changes will happen to you, too.

Here Are 6 Helpful Tips Concerning Your Dreams And Goals

1. *Invest One Hour In Writing Down Clearly The Goals That Really Matter To You At This Point.* Keep it confidential and private. "Write the vision,

and make it plain upon tables, that he may run that readeth it" (Hab. 2:2).

2. *Permit Unexciting Dreams Of Yesterday To Die.* Stop pursuing something that does not have the ability to excite you anymore. Don't feel obligated to keep trying to obtain it...if you are in a different place in your life (see Isa. 43:18,19).

3. *Do Not Depend On Others To Understand Your Dreams And Goals.* Permit them their individuality, also. They have every right to love the things they love. But refuse to be intimidated by their efforts to persuade you to move in a different direction with your life.

4. *Never Make Permanent Decisions Because Of Temporary Feelings.* One young lady got so excited about a new friend, she dropped the lease on her own apartment and moved into the apartment of her friend. Within a week, she realized her mistake!

5. *Avoid Intimate Relationships With Those Who Do Not Really Respect Your Dreams.* You will have to sever ties. Wrong people do not always leave your life voluntarily. Life is too short to permit discouragers close to you. "And have no fellowship with the unfruitful works of darkness, but rather reprove them" (Eph. 5:11).

6. *Anticipate Changes In Your Goals.* Your present feelings and opinions are not permanent. New experiences are coming. New relationships are ahead. Stay conscious of this.

When you assess and evaluate your goals, you will unclutter your life of the unnecessary.

That's one of the Secrets of Productivity.

≈ 2 ≈

INVEST WHATEVER IS NECESSARY TO CREATE THE ATMOSPHERE THAT MOTIVATES YOU.

Motivation Requires Climate.
Your surroundings are so important. Your atmosphere must receive your attention. It will not happen automatically. You must control the atmosphere around your life or it will control you.

10 Facts In Creating The Climate And Atmosphere You Need

1. *Your Climate Influences The Decisions You Make.* When you are in a high fashion clothing store, the music is often quiet, classical, or dignified. When you go into a store where the younger generation makes purchases, the music is fast, upbeat, and energizing. The merchants have created an environment that influences you to buy.

2. *Your Surroundings Contain Colors That Affect You Emotionally.* Many years ago, I read where a certain shade of pink was used in prisons to reduce violence and fights. Some say that

bodybuilders can lose one third of their ability if they look at a pink wall while they work out. Colors affect us. Colors affect our strength, our enthusiasm and the decisions we make.

3. *Everyone Needs Something Different Around Them.* You must discern what environment and atmosphere brings out the best in you.

When I need energy and must move quickly from project to project, I love to listen to praise music that is energizing and exciting. When I want to ponder and reflect, I love to listen to slower, more worshipful music. I know the value of protecting the climate around myself.

4. *Nobody Else Can Create Your Atmosphere For You.* You must discern it and pursue it for yourself.

5. *What You See Controls What You Desire.* When you see a billboard advertising hamburgers, you suddenly experience a desire for hamburgers. That's why you must put around yourself pictures and images of the things you want.

6. *What You Are Viewing Daily Affects What You Desire To Do.* When children see the playground at McDonald's, they are suddenly inspired to stop everything and go play.

7. *Photographs Of Things You Want In Your Future Should Be Kept Visible At All Times.* It may be a boat you want to buy, a home you want to live in or a picture of yourself 20 pounds lighter. These images are influencing *the direction* your decisions will take you.

8. *Your Investment In Interior Decorating Can Make A Huge Difference In Your Productivity.*

A new rug, a picture on the wall, a vase with a rose, every small thing can increase the warmth and caring of your environment.

9. *Experimentation To Discover What You Really Need Around You Is Permissible.* It is wonderful to explore variations of climates and environments. An interior decorator, the suggestions of a friend or your own personal visits to different stores can help you discover the atmosphere you prefer to work in, play around or simply relax and rest in. Each atmosphere produces a different emotion.

10. *Do Not Wait For Others To Initiate Changes In Your Environment.* Make any investment necessary to create the kind of environment that inspires you toward excellence and the improvement of your life.

Sculpturing an environment that specifically motivates you is an important key to uncommon productivity.

RECOMMENDED BOOKS:
Secrets Of The Richest Man Who Ever Lived (B-99/$10)
Seeds Of Wisdom On Goal-Setting (B-125/$5)

Any Movement Towards
Order Generates Pleasure.

-MIKE MURDOCK

❦ **3** ❦

HABITUALIZE ORDER.

Success Comes Through Small Steps.
Order and organizing your life is one of these important steps.

11 Important Facts About Order And Organizing Your Life

1. *Order Is The Accurate Arrangement Of Things.* Order is placing an item where it belongs. Order is keeping your shirts, ties and shoes in the appropriate place in your closet.

2. *You Were Created For Order.* Anything that slows you down emotionally or mentally will become a distraction.

3. *Order Increases Comfort.* When you walk into a room of order, you want to *stay.* Things are "right." You feel clean, energized and happy. When you walk into a room of clutter and disorder, an unexplainable agitation begins. Perhaps you cannot even name it or understand it.

4. *When You Increase Order In Your Life, You Will Increase Your Productivity.* Filing cabinets, trays on the desk, and special places for folders make it easier to get your job done *on time.*

5. *Order Eliminates Stress And Agitation.* Have you ever shuffled paper after paper in search

of a bill? Of course! When you finally located the bill, you were agitated and angry. It affected your entire day. *Disorder influences your attitude more than you could ever imagine.*

6. *Everything You Are Doing Is Affecting Order In Your Life.* Think for a moment. You get up from your breakfast table. Either you will leave your plate on the table, or you will take it to the sink. The decision you make will either increase the order or disorder around you. (Leaving it on the table increases your work load and creates disorder. Taking it to the sink *immediately* brings *order.*)

It happened last night for me. I took off my suit coat and laid it over the chair. I didn't really feel like taking it over to the closet and hanging it up. However, realizing that I was going to have hang it up sooner or later, I walked over to the closet and hung up my coat. *I increased order* around myself immediately.

▶ Every *moment* you are increasing order or creating disorder around your life.

▶ Small tiny actions can eventually produce chaotic situations.

7. *Every Person Around You Is Increasing Order Or Disorder.* Some people have an *attitude* of disorder. They are unhappy unless everything is in disarray and cluttered. Others refuse to work in such an environment. Their productivity requires organization.

8. *Recognize The Long-Term Chaos And Losses That Disorder Will Create.* If this continues, your momentum will eventually destroy you and

your productivity. Successes will become fewer.

9. *Take A Long, Hard And Serious Look At Your Personality And What You Can Do To Take Steps Toward Change.* Be honest. Evaluate your personal weaknesses.

10. *Ask Others Who Are Gifted In Organization To Assist You And Keep You On Course.* I read where Donald Trump, the billionaire, said that he hired one woman whose only job is to keep things in order around him.

11. *Recognize Those Who God Puts Close To You Who Can Correct Things Around You And Keep Things In Order.* Request their assistance and encouragement.

Do not try to justify yourself. Relax.

Take a small, tiny step today toward putting things around you in order.

It is commendable that you are planning to take an entire week of your vacation to put everything in order in your house next summer. However, I suggest you begin *this very moment* taking some steps to put things in place there in your room!

Just 20 minutes can make a major difference. Little hinges swing big doors. *You Can Get Anywhere You Want To Go If You Are Willing To Take Enough Small Steps.* Move toward order.

Only one thing is greater than order...the *Habit* of Order. It's a powerful secret to maintaining *continuous* productivity.

What You Can Tolerate
You Cannot Change.

-MIKE MURDOCK

❧ 4 ❧

NEVER DO WHAT A MACHINE CAN DO.

Proper Equipment Increases Your Productivity.

Never have someone do a job that a machine can do instead. This is a humorous explanation of the advantages of proper machines.

10 Advantages In Using Appropriate Technology

1. Machines Do Not *Require Coaxing,* Just Repair.

2. Machines Do Not Get *Discouraged* When Their Mother-in-law Comes To Town.

3. Machines Are Never *Disloyal*, Discussing Your Secrets With Everyone Else.

4. Your Machines Will Not *File Grievance Reports* Against You When You Fail To Meet Their Expectations.

5. Machines Do Not Require *Medical Insurance,* Sick Leave Or Time Off.

6. Machines Can Be *Replaced* Quickly And Easily Without Breaking Your Heart.

7. Machines Do Not *Request A Retirement*

Fund And Want To Be Paid For The Years Ahead When They Do Not Perform.

8.   Machines Never Come To Work *Late* And Want To *Leave Early*.

9.   Machines Will Work *Through* Lunch, Requiring No "Break Time."

10. Machines Never Interrupt The Productivity Of *Other Machines,* Slowing Down The Entire Project.

6 Keys To Using Equipment For Increasing Your Productivity

1.   *Find The Most Effective Equipment Possible To Do Your Present Job.*

2.   *Telephone Other Businesses Or Companies To Locate Appropriate Or Needed Machines And Equipment.*

3.   *Attend Seminars And Workshops That Increase Your Efficiency Or Skills On Computers And Other Machines.*

4.   *Tell Your Boss The Equipment Necessary To Do The Job More Efficiently, More Accurately And Quickly.* (He will usually do anything possible to make the hours of employees more effective and productive.)

5.   *Continuously Evaluate Your Work Speed.* What is slowing you down? What machine could make a big difference in the completion of your daily tasks and responsibilities?

6.   *Present Your Supervisors With Options, Costs And Potential Benefits Of Purchasing More Machines.* Your boss will treasure it and learn to appreciate his own work load reduction because of

it. It decreases the opportunities for mistakes. It increases your sense of progress and accomplishment.

Search for appropriate equipment to accomplish your tasks quickly.

Appropriate equipment can increase your productivity 10 times.

You Will Only Be Pursued
For The Problems
You Solve.

-MIKE MURDOCK

⇜ 5 ⇝

ALWAYS KEEP A SMALL TAPE RECORDER IN YOUR HAND.

Talking Is Faster Than Writing.
Someone has said that you can talk four times faster than you can write. I *always* keep note paper and pen handy. *Always.* But, it is far easier and more productive to dictate into a little tape recorder than it is to write longhand on my legal pad. (Admittedly, some of my handwritten notes excite me more when I can see them written large in my own handwriting using a black pen.) But, when there is a flood of ideas and thoughts pouring through me, I consider the small tape recorder to be a gift from God. Every achiever should own and use one.

I have only known two friends in my entire life who keep a microcassette recorder with them at all times. Others claim to have them "somewhere in my office." Or somewhere "down here in my briefcase." But, they are not accustomed to using a recorder on a continuous basis.

4 Facts To Remember About Dictation

1. *Recording Frees Your Mind From The Stress Of Memory.* When you want to remember

something, you may find yourself continuously replaying it over and over in your mind, so you will not forget it. Consequently, your mind cannot be free for conversation, a great *idea* or unusual creativity. Why? Because subconsciously you are trying to *remember* something you need to do or delegate.

We try everything to help us remember. We keep lists, tie strings around our fingers, post notes. But, when you create the habit of keeping a microcassette recorder with you *every moment* of your life, you will began to produce ten times more than ever before. It has worked for me!

2. *Develop The Habit Of Keeping Your Recorder Conveniently Close.* It may be uncomfortable, initially. When I first started keeping my microcassette in my pocket, it seemed a little odd and awkward, even cumbersome. However, once I saw the many pages of material dictating produced, it became a joy. This wonderful tool was a constant reminder that great thoughts and ideas were flowing through me all day.

3. *Making Your Moments Productive Is One Of The Greatest Secrets Of Life.* Thousands keep waiting for a time that they are going to take off a few days or weeks and produce a book, plan a project or design their house. Fifty years can go by without any of it ever occurring, unless you understand how to *turn each moment into a miracle.*

4. *Use Your Recorder Daily.*

Always Keep A Small Tape Recorder In Your Hand. *That is One of the most important Golden Secrets of Productivity you can learn.*

❦ 6 ❧

VERIFY EVERY INSTRUCTION.

Confirm Everything.

I have marveled how so many have kept their jobs over the years. Few seem to *follow-through* on instructions given to them by their supervisors.

True, there are a few close to you who may have proven themselves over a long period of time. They understand you. They are diligent, aggressive and trustworthy. But my own experience is that there are *less than five people* in your life that you can count on to *fully complete an assigned task with excellence on the schedule you requested.*

4 Qualities Of An Uncommon Employee

1. *They Keep Paper And Pen In Their Hand.* Never trust an employee who does not regularly carry paper and pen in their hand to follow through on something you have asked them to do. *Never.* They trust their memory and want you to trust it also.

2. *They Always Reach For Paper And Pen To Document The Instruction.* They don't simply nod. They *write* it down. They *document* it. They don't trust their memory. Bank on it—the instruction

will be *completed* even in their busyness.

3. *They Ask Additional Questions About The Assignment Or Instruction.* Few instructions are complete at the beginning. Uncommon employees ask:

> a. Is there a *deadline* on this?
> b. When do you need a *report back* on the results of this telephone call?
> c. Is there anything *additional* I should know about?

When additional questions are never asked by an employee, *they are not giving any thought to the instructions.*

4. *They Always Reply, "I will do it, sir."* Believe me, they get to it. They don't "*try.*" They do it.

7 Things You Should Remember When You Delegate Instructions To Others

1. Communicate Clearly *The Importance* Of The Instruction.

2. Give The Instruction To *One Person* Only.

3. *Document The Date* You Gave The Instruction.

4. Require A Continuous *Progress Report.*

5. *Agree* Upon The Expected Deadline For The Completion Of The Task.

6. Never Give An Instruction To Someone *Incapable Of Completing It.*

7. Never *Assume* Your Instructions Have Been Completed. Follow through.

It's one of the Secrets of Uncommon Productivity.

➣ 7 ➣

ANTICIPATE AND AVOID UNNECESSARY CONFLICT.

➣▬◗▬◖▬

Most Battles Are Not Really Important.

Here Are 16 Important Facts About Conflicts And Contentious People

1. *Conflict Distracts You From Your Dreams And Goals.* A contentious person often considers himself very honest and up front. In fact, they usually take pride in telling you "the way things really are." Subconsciously, they are often modeling someone in their life (a father or mother) who accomplished their goals through *intimidation.* Subconsciously, they admire this person and have decided to follow that pattern, failing to see the losses created through this kind of attitude.

2. *Nothing Is More Harmful To A Company Than A Contentious Employee.* Every boss knows this. When an employee cannot get along with other employees, profits are lost. That employee becomes costly. Focus is broken. Other employees become emotionally fragmented. Important projects are delayed.

3. *Contentious   People   Destroy   The*

Momentum, Bonding And Synergy That Agreement Can Create. "Mark them which cause divisions and offenses...avoid them" (Romans 16:17).

"And the servant of the Lord must not strive; but be gentle unto all men, apt to teach, patient," (2 Tim. 2:24).

4. *Contentious People Are In Total Opposition To The Law Of Agreement, The Greatest Law Of Success On Earth.* "Two are better than one; because they have a good reward for their labour. For if they fall, the one will lift up his fellow: but woe to him that is alone when he falleth; for he hath not another to help him up" (Eccl. 4:9,10).

5. *The Character Of A Contentious Person Is Only Revealed When You Rebuke Them.* If he is a scorner and fool, he will hate you. If he is a wise person simply needing correction, he will love you. "Reprove not a scorner, lest he hate thee: rebuke a wise man, and he will love thee" (Prov. 9:8).

6. *Contentious People Discuss Situations That Do Not Involve Them.* This is one of the evidences of a contentious person. They discuss the business of others. "He that passeth by, and meddleth with strife belonging not to him, is like one that taketh a dog by the ears" (Prov. 26:17).

7. *A Contentious Person Enjoys Debate, Disputings And Opposing Whatever Has Been Spoken.* A contentious person always looks for a reason to disagree about something. They *ignore* every point of *agreement.*

8. *A Contentious Person Is Always A Door For Satan To Launch Every Evil Work In An*

Organization. "For where envying and strife is, there is confusion and every evil work" (James 3:16).

9. *A Contentious Person Is In Opposition To Godly Wisdom.* "But the Wisdom that is from above is first pure, then peaceable, gentle, and easy to be intreated, full of mercy and good fruits, without partiality, and without hypocrisy" (James 3:17).

10. *A Contentious Attitude And Spirit Is Always Birthed By Unthankfulness.* It is a sin that God abhors. Unthankfulness was the first sin ever committed. Satan was unthankful for his position and chose to fight for a change. *Ingratitude is poisonous.* It can destroy a family within weeks. It can ruin a successful organization within months. Churches exploding with growth have fragmented within weeks when a spirit of ingratitude infected the congregation.

11. *Any Contentious Conversation Must Be Boldly Faced And Stopped Immediately.* Interrupt the conversation with, "It's wonderful how God will *turn this* for our good! I am so thankful for what He is about to do! Don't we have a wonderful God!" It will be like throwing cold water on a destructive fire.

12. *The Contentious Person Must Be Confronted Honestly And Courageously About Their Attitude.* Others are bold enough to poison your climate and atmosphere with Arrows of Unthankfulness piercing the air. So, dominate your turf. Take charge. Use your words to turn the tide.

13. *Contentious People Often Sabotage The*

Work Of God. Many years ago I heard one of the most startling statements from a famous missionary. I was sitting under some huge trees in East Africa. Monkeys were jumping from tree limb to tree limb. My precious missionary friend explained the number one reason some missionaries never fulfill their full term on the field. (I thought missionaries came home due to sickness, culture shock or lack of finances.)

"Mike, the number one reason missionaries do not stay on the mission field is their *inability to get along with the other missionaries.*" Think about it. Missionaries who should be obsessed with sharing the Gospel, often return home because of the *failure to create an environment of agreement.*

14. *Contention Is Contagious.* When someone permits the spirit of conflict and disputing to enter their life, they will influence and affect *everyone around them.* I have seen a happy, peaceful household dissolve into arguments within 30 minutes of the arrival of a contentious person. That person *carried* the spirit of contention with them.

15. *Any Contentious Person Who Refuses To Change Must Not Continue To Have Access To You.* "Where no wood is, there the fire goeth out: so where there is no talebearer, the strife ceaseth. As coals are to burning coals, and wood to fire; so is a contentious man to kindle strife" (Prov. 26:20,21). *Your attitude is a personal decision.* Your attitude is a *mood* created by your chosen *focus.*

16. *You Cannot Succeed In An Environment Of Strife.* "It is better to dwell in the corner of the

housetop, than with a brawling woman and in a wide house" (Prov. 25:24).

Remember, conflict always begins with a person, not merely an issue (Prov. 26:20).

Agreement is the greatest enemy Satan has ever faced. Walk away from contentious people.

Strife is an Enemy to Productivity.

Peace is the invisible climate that multiplies your productivity.

My Special Prayer:

"Holy Spirit, you have designed our Assignment. Expose any enemy to it. Increase our productivity...for the sake of the gospel. In Jesus' name. Amen."

RECOMMENDED BOOKS:
The Assignment: The Dream & The Destiny (B-74/$10)
The Assignment: The Anointing & The Adversity (B-75/$10)
The Assignment: The Trials & The Triumphs (B-97/$10)
The Assignment: The Pain & The Passion (B-98/$10)

DR. MIKE MURDOCK

1 Has embraced his Assignment to Pursue...Proclaim...and Publish the Wisdom of God to help people achieve their dreams and goals.

2 Began full-time evangelism at the age of 19, which has continued since 1966.

3 Has traveled and spoken to more than 14,000 audiences in 38 countries, including East and West Africa, the Orient and Europe.

4 Noted author of 120 books, including best sellers, "Wisdom For Winning," "Dream Seeds" and "The Double Diamond Principle."

5 Created the popular "Topical Bible" series for Businessmen, Mothers, Fathers, Teenagers; "The One-Minute Pocket Bible" series, and "The Uncommon Life" series.

6 Has composed more than 5,700 songs such as "I Am Blessed," "You Can Make It," "God Rides On Wings Of Love" and "Jesus, Just The Mention Of Your Name," recorded by many gospel artists.

7 Is the Founder of The Wisdom Center, in Denton, Texas.

8 Has a weekly television program called *"Wisdom Keys With Mike Murdock."*

9 Has appeared often on TBN, CBN and other television network programs.

10 Is a Founding Trustee on the Board of International Charismatic Bible Ministries with Oral Roberts.

11 Has had more than 3,500 accept the call into full-time ministry under his ministry.

THE MINISTRY

1 **Wisdom Books & Literature** Over 120 best-selling Wisdom Books and 70 Teaching Tape Series.

2 **Church Crusades** - Multitudes are ministered to in crusades and seminars throughout America in "The Uncommon Wisdom Conference." Known as a man who loves pastors has focused on church crusades for 36 years.

3 **Music Ministry** - Millions have been blessed by the anointed songwriting and singing of Mike Murdock, who has made over 15 music albums and CDs available.

4 **Television** - *"Wisdom Keys With Mike Murdock,"* a nationally-syndicated weekly television program features Mike Murdock's teaching and music.

5 **The Wisdom Center** - The Ministry Offices where Dr. Murdock holds an annual School of Wisdom for those desiring "The Uncommon Life."

6 **Schools of the Holy Spirit** - Mike Murdock hosts Schools of the Holy Spirit in many churches to mentor believers on the Person and companionship of the Holy Spirit.

7 **Schools of Wisdom** - In 24 major cities Mike Murdock hosts Saturday Schools of Wisdom for those who want personalized and advanced training for achieving "The Uncommon Life."

8 **Missionary Ministry** - Dr Mike. Murdock's overseas outreaches to 38 countries have included crusades in East and West Africa, South America and Europe.

DECISION

Will You Accept Jesus As Your Personal Savior Today?

The Bible says, "That if thou shalt confess with thy mouth the Lord Jesus, and shalt believe in thine heart that God hath raised Him from the dead, thou shalt be saved" (Rom. 10:9).

Pray this prayer from your heart today!

"Dear Jesus, I believe that you died for me and rose again on the third day. I confess I am a sinner...I need Your love and forgiveness...Come into my heart. Forgive my sins. I receive Your eternal life. Confirm Your love by giving me peace, joy and supernatural love for others. Amen."

DR. MIKE MURDOCK

is in tremendous demand as one of the most dynamic speakers in America today.

More than 14,000 audiences in 38 countries have attended his meetings and seminars. Hundreds of invitations come to him from churches, colleges, and business corporations. He is a noted author of over 130 books, including the best sellers, *"The Leadership Secrets of Jesus"* and *"Secrets of the Richest Man Who Ever Lived."* Thousands view his weekly television program, *"Wisdom Keys with Mike Murdock."* Many attend his Saturday School of Wisdom Breakfasts that he hosts in major cities of America.

Yes, Mike! I made a decision to accept Christ as my personal Savior today. Please send me my free gift of your book, *"31 Keys to a New Beginning"* to help me with my new life in Christ. *(B-48)*

NAME   BIRTHDAY

ADDRESS

CITY   STATE   ZIP

PHONE   E-MAIL   B-137
Mail form to:

The Wisdom Center · P. O. Box 99 · Denton, TX 76202
1-888-WISDOM-1 (1-888-947-3661) · Website: ***www.thewisdomcenter.cc***

ORDER FORM THE WISDOM CENTER

(All books paperback unless indicated otherwise.)

Qty	Code	Book Title	USA	Total
	B-01	Wisdom For Winning	$10	
	B-02	Five Steps Out Of Depression	$ 3	
	B-03	The Sex Trap	$ 3	
	B-04	Ten Lies People Believe About Money	$ 3	
	B-05	Finding Your Purpose In Life	$ 3	
	B-06	Creating Tomorrow Through Seed-Faith	$ 3	
	B-07	Battle Techniques For War Weary Saints	$ 3	
	B-08	Enjoying The Winning Life	$ 3	
	B-09	Four Forces/Guarantee Career Success	$ 3	
	B-10	The Bridge Called Divorce	$ 3	
	B-11	Dream Seeds	$ 9	
	B-12	The Ministers Encyclopedia, Vol. 1	$20	
	B-13	Seeds Of Wisdom On Dreams And Goals, Vol. 1	$ 3	
	B-14	Seeds Of Wisdom On Relationships, Vol. 2	$ 3	
	B-15	Seeds Of Wisdom On Miracles, Vol. 3	$ 3	
	B-16	Seeds Of Wisdom On Seed-Faith, Vol. 4	$ 3	
	B-17	Seeds Of Wisdom On Overcoming, Vol. 5	$ 3	
	B-18	Seeds Of Wisdom On Habits, Vol. 6	$ 3	
	B-19	Seeds Of Wisdom On Warfare, Vol. 7	$ 3	
	B-20	Seeds Of Wisdom On Obedience, Vol. 8	$ 3	
	B-21	Seeds Of Wisdom On Adversity, Vol. 9	$ 3	
	B-22	Seeds Of Wisdom On Prosperity, Vol. 10	$ 3	
	B-23	Seeds Of Wisdom On Prayer, Vol. 11	$ 3	
	B-24	Seeds Of Wisdom On Faith-Talk, Vol. 12	$ 3	
	B-25	7 Kinds Of People You Cannot Help	$ 5	
	B-26	The God Book	$10	
	B-27	The Jesus Book	$10	
	B-28	The Blessing Bible	$10	
	B-29	The Survival Bible	$10	
	B-30	The Teens Topical Bible	$ 8	
	B-31	Seeds Of Wisdom Topical Bible	$15	
	B-32	The Minister's Topical Bible	$ 8	
	B-33	The Businessman's Topical Bible	$ 8	
	B-34	The Grandparent's Topical Bible	$ 8	
	B-35	The Father's Topical Bible	$ 8	
	B-36	The Mother's Topical Bible	$ 8	
	B-37	The New Believer's Topical Bible	$ 8	
	B-38	The Widow's Topical Bible	$ 8	
	B-39	The Double Diamond Principle	$ 9	
	B-40	Wisdom For Crisis Times	$ 9	
	B-41	The Gift Of Wisdom, Vol. 1	$10	
	B-42	One-Minute Businessman's Devotional	$12	
	B-43	One-Minute Businesswoman's Devotional	$12	
	B-44	31 Secrets For Career Success	$10	
	B-45	101 Wisdom Keys	$ 5	
	B-46	31 Facts About Wisdom	$ 5	
	B-47	The Covenant Of The Fifty-Eight Blessings	$ 8	
	B-48	31 Keys To A New Beginning	$ 5	
	B-49	The Proverbs 31 Woman	$ 7	
	B-50	One-Minute Pocket Bible For The Achiever	$ 5	
	B-51	One-Minute Pocket Bible For Fathers	$ 5	
	B-52	One-Minute Pocket Bible For Mothers	$ 5	
	B-53	One-Minute Pocket Bible For Teenagers	$ 5	
	B-54	31 Greatest Chapters In The Bible	$10	
	B-55	20 Keys To A Happier Marriage	$ 3	
	B-56	How To Turn Mistakes Into Miracles	$ 3	

Qty	Code	Book Title	USA	Total
	B-57	31 Secrets Of An Unforgettable Woman	$ 9	
	B-58	The Mentors Manna On Attitude	$ 3	
	B-59	The Making Of A Champion	$10	
	B-60	One-Minute Pocket Bible For Men	$ 5	
	B-61	One-Minute Pocket Bible For Women	$ 5	
	B-62	One-Minute Pocket Bible/Bus.Professionals	$ 5	
	B-63	One-Minute Pocket Bible For Truckers	$ 5	
	B-64	Seven Obstacles To Abundant Success	$ 3	
	B-65	Born To Taste The Grapes	$ 3	
	B-66	Greed, Gold And Giving	$ 3	
	B-67	Gift Of Wisdom For Champions	$10	
	B-68	Gift Of Wisdom For Achievers	$10	
	B-69	Wisdom Keys For A Powerful Prayer Life	$ 3	
	B-70	Gift Of Wisdom For Mothers	$10	
	B-71	Wisdom - God's Golden Key To Success	$ 7	
	B-72	The Double Diamond Daily Devotional	$15	
	B-73	The Mentors Manna On Abilities	$ 3	
	B-74	The Assignment: Dream/Destiny, Vol. 1	$10	
	B-75	The Assignment: Anointing/Adversity, Vol. 2	$10	
	B-76	The Mentors Manna On Assignment	$ 3	
	B-77	The Gift Of Wisdom For Fathers	$10	
	B-78	The Mentors Manna On The Secret Place	$ 3	
	B-79	The Mentors Manna On Achievement	$ 3	
	B-80	The Greatest Success Habit On Earth	$ 3	
	B-81	The Mentors Manna On Adversity	$ 3	
	B-82	31 Reasons People Do Not Receive Their Financial Harvest	$12	
	B-83	The Gift Of Wisdom For Wives	$10	
	B-84	The Gift Of Wisdom For Husbands	$10	
	B-85	The Gift Of Wisdom For Teenagers	$10	
	B-86	The Gift Of Wisdom For Leaders	$10	
	B-87	The Gift Of Wisdom For Graduates	$10	
	B-88	The Gift Of Wisdom For Brides	$10	
	B-89	The Gift Of Wisdom For Grooms	$10	
	B-90	The Gift Of Wisdom For Ministers	$10	
	B-91	The Leadership Secrets Of Jesus	$10	
	B-92	Secrets Of The Journey, Vol. 1	$ 5	
	B-93	Secrets Of The Journey, Vol. 2	$ 5	
	B-94	Secrets Of The Journey, Vol. 3	$ 5	
	B-95	Secrets Of The Journey, Vol. 4	$ 5	
	B-96	Secrets Of The Journey, Vol. 5	$ 5	
	B-97	The Assignment: Trials/Triumphs, Vol. 3	$ 5	
	B-98	The Assignment: Pain/Passion, Vol. 4	$ 5	
	B-99	Secrets Of The Richest Man Who Ever Lived	$10	
	B-100	The Holy Spirit Handbook, Vol. 1	$10	
	B-101	The 3 Most Important Things In Your Life	$10	
	B-102	Secrets Of The Journey, Vol. 6	$ 5	
	B-103	Secrets Of The Journey, Vol. 7	$ 5	
	B-104	7 Days To 1000 Times More	$10	
	B-105	31 Days To Succeeding On Your Job	$10	
	B-106	The Uncommon Leader	$ 5	
	B-107	The Uncommon Minister, Vol. 1	$ 5	
	B-108	The Uncommon Minister, Vol. 2	$ 5	
	B-109	The Uncommon Minister, Vol. 3	$ 5	
	B-110	The Uncommon Minister, Vol. 4	$ 5	
	B-111	The Uncommon Minister, Vol. 5	$ 5	
	B-112	The Uncommon Minister, Vol. 6	$ 5	
	B-113	The Uncommon Minister, Vol. 7	$ 5	

Qty	Code	Book Title	USA	Total
	B-114	The Law Of Recognition	$10	
	B-115	Seeds Of Wisdom On The Secret Place, Vol. 13	$ 5	
	B-116	Seeds Of Wisdom On The Holy Spirit, Vol. 14	$ 5	
	B-117	Seeds Of Wisdom On The Word Of God, Vol. 15	$ 5	
	B-118	Seeds Of Wisdom On Problem Solving, Vol. 16	$ 5	
	B-119	Seeds Of Wisdom On Favor, Vol. 17	$ 5	
	B-120	Seeds Of Wisdom On Healing, Vol. 18	$ 5	
	B-121	Seeds Of Wisdom On Time-Management, Vol. 19	$ 5	
	B-122	Seeds Of Wisdom On Your Assignment, Vol. 20	$ 5	
	B-123	Seeds Of Wisdom On Financial Breakthrough, Vol. 21	$ 5	
	B-124	Seeds Of Wisdom On Enemies, Vol. 22	$ 5	
	B-125	Seeds Of Wisdom On Decision-Making, Vol. 23	$ 5	
	B-126	Seeds Of Wisdom On Mentorship Vol. 24	$ 5	
	B-127	Seeds Of Wisdom On Goal-Setting, Vol. 25	$ 5	
	B-128	Seeds Of Wisdom On The Power Of Words, Vol. 26	$ 5	
	B-129	The Secret Of The Seed	$10	
	B-130	The Uncommon Millionaire, Vol. 1	$10	
	B-131	The Uncommon Father	$ 8	
	B-132	The Uncommon Mother	$ 8	
	B-133	The Uncommon Achiever	$10	
	B-134	The Uncommon Armorbearer	$10	
	B-135	The Uncommon Dream, Vol. 1	$10	
	B-136	The Wisdom Commentary, Vol 1 (Seed-gift)	$100	

☐ CASH   ☐ CHECK   ☐ MONEY ORDER   ☐ VISA

CREDIT CARD # ☐ MC   ☐ DISCOVER ☐ AMEX

EXPIRATION DATE [ ] [ ] [ ] [ ]   SORRY NO C.OD's

SIGNATURE _____

TOTAL PAGES 1, 2, 3	$
SHIPPING ADD 10%-USA/20%-OTHERS	$
CANADA CURRENCY DIFFERENCE ADD 20%	$
TOTAL ENCLOSED	$

PLEASE PRINT

Name _____

Address _____

City _____ State _____ Zip _____

Phone (____) _____

E-mail _____

Mail to: **The Wisdom Center** • P.O. Box 99 • Denton, TX 76202
1-888-WISDOM-1 (1-888-947-3661) • Website: **thewisdomcenter.cc**

My Gift Of Appreciation...

The Wisdom Commentary

The Wisdom Commentary includes
52 topics...for mentoring your
family every week of the year.

These topics include:

- Abilities
- Achievement
- Anointing
- Assignment
- Bitterness
- Blessing
- Career
- Change
- Children
- Dating
- Depression
- Discipline
- Divorce
- Dreams And Goals
- Enemy
- Enthusiasm
- Favor
- Finances
- Fools

- Giving
- Goal-Setting
- God
- Happiness
- Holy Spirit
- Ideas
- Intercession
- Jobs
- Loneliness
- Love
- Mentorship
- Ministers
- Miracles
- Mistakes
- Money
- Negotiation
- Prayer
- Problem-Solving
- Protégés

- Satan
- Secret Place
- Seed-Faith
- Self-Confidence
- Struggle
- Success
- Time-Management
- Understanding
- Victory
- Weaknesses
- Wisdom
- Word Of God
- Words
- Work

**GIFT OF APPRECIATION
For Your
Sponsorship
Seed of $100
or More
B-136
GIFT OF APPRECIATION**

My Gift Of Appreciation To My Sponsors!
...Those Who Sponsor One Square Foot In
The Completion Of The Wisdom Center!

Thank you so much for becoming a part of this wonderful project...The completion of The Wisdom Center.
The total purchase and renovation cost of this facility (10,000 square feet) is just over $1,000,000. This
approximately $100 per square foot. **The Wisdom Commentary is my Gift of Appreciation for you
Sponsorship Seed of $100...that sponsors one square foot of The Wisdom Center. Become a Sponsor!** You
will love this Volume 1, of The Wisdom Commentary. It is my exclusive Gift of Appreciation for The Wisdo
Key Family who partners with me in the Work of God as a Sponsor.

THE WISDOM CENTER P.O. Box 99, Denton, Texas 76202

Website:
WWW.THEWISDOMCENTER.CC

1-888-WISDOM
(1-888-947-366)

My Gift Of Appreciation...
The *Wisdom Commentary*

The Wisdom Commentary includes 52 topics...for mentoring your family every week of the year.

My Gift Of Appreciation To My Sponsors!
...Those Who Sponsor One Square Foot In The Completion Of The Wisdom Center!

Order from our website: **www.thewisdomcenter.cc**

GIFT APPRECIATION

For Your Sponsorship Seed of $100 or More
B136

Order Today!
1-888-WISDOM-1
(1-888-947-3661)

The Wisdom Center
P.O. Box 99
Denton, Texas 76202
www.thewisdomcenter.cc

THE WISDOM CENTER

1-888-WISDOM-1 *(1-888-947-3661)*

Mon.-Fri.
8 AM-5 PM CST

visit us at:
www.thewisdomcenter.cc

PRODUCT NUMBER	PRODUCT DESCRIPTION	QTY	PRICE	TOTAL
				1
				2
				3
				4
				5
				6
		SubTotal. $		7
		Canada ADD 20% $		8
		S/H Add 10% $		9
		TOTAL $		10
		My Seed Offering $		11

Name

Address

City _____ State _____ Zip

Phone _____ Email

Method of Payment
☐ Cash ☐ Check ☐ Visa ☐ MC ☐ Amex ☐ Discover

Card#

Birthday ___ MO ___ DAY   Expiration Date

Total Enclosed $ _____   Signature

(Sorry No C.O.D's)

B-137

DISCOUNTS
Bookstore/Distributors

QTY.	DISCOUNT	
	Retail	
1-9		
10-499	40%	
500-1999	50%	
2000-4999	60%	
5000 & Up	Contact Office	

(single titles only)

My Dear Partner,

Your Productivity Matters To God.

Your Rewards depend on your accomplishments.

...He will reward every man according to his works. (See Matthew 16:27)

In fact, a divine death sentence is pronounced on anything that does not generate increase. (Luke 13:7 Matthew 25:15)

Productivity generates joy.

Productivity unleashes favor with others.

Productivity guarantees promotion.

Productivity is necessary for surviving The Earth Experience.

That's why I wrote this book "just for you". Teach this to your family, associates and those whose success truly matters to you. The Person of Jesus creates your Peace. The Principles of Jesus creates your Prosperity.

Write me your special prayer needs. You can depend on my prayers for you.

Your Faithful Intercessor,

Mike Murdock

P. S. Your Seed into this ministry will unleash Uncommon Increase...wherever you need it most. Sow joyfully...generously...expectantly when you write me this week!

Somebody's Future
Will Not Begin Until You Enter.

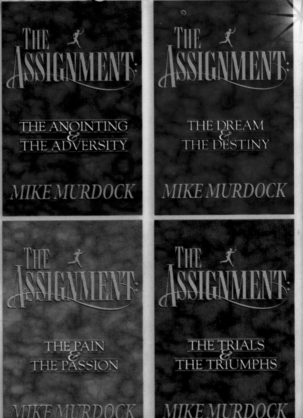

THIS COLLECTION INCLUDES 4 DIFFERENT BOOKS CONTAINING UNCOMMON WISDOM FOR DISCOVERING YOUR LIFE ASSIGNMENT

▸ How To Achieve A God-Given Dream And Goal

▸ How To Know Who Is Assigned To You

▸ The Purpose And Rewards Of An Enemy

Wisdom Is The Principal Thing

Book Pak
WBL-14 / **$30**

Buy 3-Get 1 Free
($10 Each/$40 Value!)

The Wisdom Center

The Secret Place

Library Pak

Songs From The Secret Place

Over 40 Great Songs On 6 Music Tapes
Including "I'm In Love" / Love Songs From The Holy Spirit
Birthed In The Secret Place / Side A Is Dr. Mike Murdock
Singing / Side B Is Music Only For Your Personal Prayer Time

DR. MIKE MURDOCK
P.O. BOX 99 • DALLAS, TEXAS • 75221
Songs From The Secret Place

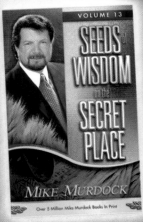

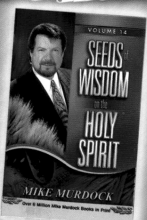

Seeds Of Wisdom On The Secret Place

4 Secrets The Holy Spirit Reveals In The Secret Place /
The Necessary Ingredients In Creating Your Secret Place /
10 Miracles That Will Happen In The Secret Place

Wisdom Is The Principal Thing
Book/Tape Pak
SP PAK-001 /$30
Six Audio Tapes & Two Books
(A $40 Value!)
The Wisdom Center

Seeds Of Wisdom On The Holy Spirit

The Protocol For Entering The Presence Of The Holy Spirit /
The Greatest Day Of My Life And What Made It So /
Power Keys For Developing Your Personal Relationship With The Holy Spirit

The Wisdom Center

ORDER TODAY!
www.thewisdomcenter.cc

1-888-WISDOM-1
(1-888-947-3661)

THE WISDOM CENTER • P.O. Box 99 • Denton, Texas 76202

E

Getting Past The Pain.

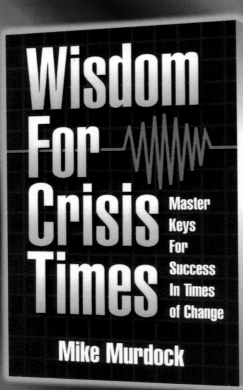

Master
Keys
For
Success
In Times
of Change

Mike Murdock

▶ 6 Essential Facts That
Must Be Faced When
Recovering From Divorce

▶ 4 Forces That
Guarantee
Career Success

▶ 3 Ways Crisis Can
Help You

▶ 4 Reasons You Are
Experiencing Opposition
To Your Assignment

▶ How To Predict The
6 Seasons Of Attack On
Your Life

▶ 4 Keys That Can Shorten
Your Present Season Of
Struggle

▶ 2 Important Facts You Must
Know About Battle &
Warfare

▶ 6 Weapons Satan Uses To
Attack Marriages

Wisdom For Crisis Times will give you
the answers to the struggle you are facing
now, and any struggle you could ever face.
Dr. Murdock presents practical steps to help
you walk through your "Seasons of Fire."

▶ 96 Wisdom Keys from God's Word
will direct you into the success that God intended
for your life. This teaching will unlock the door to your personal
happiness, peace of mind, fulfillment and success.

Wisdom Is The Principal Thing

Book
B-40 / $9

Six Audio Tapes /
TS-69 / $30

The Wisdom Center

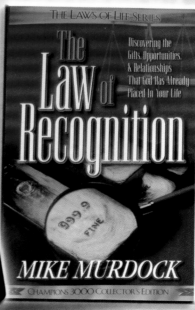

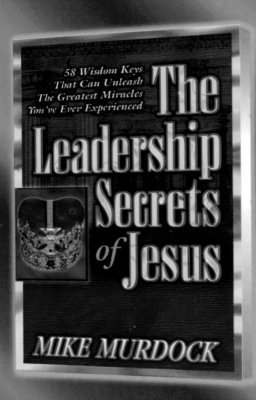

Your Rewards In Life Are Determined By The Problems You Solve.

VOLUME 16

SEEDS of WISDOM on PROBLEM SOLVING

MIKE MURDOCK

Over 6 Million Mike Murdock Books In Print

Seeds Of Wisdom On Problem Solving · Mike Murdock

- 3 Simple Ways To Increase Your Income In 90 Days
- 4 Keys To Recognizing The Problems You Were Created To Solve
- 12 Rewards Received When You Solve Problems For Others
- 5 Important Keys To Remember When You Face A Problem
- 2 Ways You Will Be Remembered
- 12 Keys to Becoming An Uncommon Problem Solver
- 6 Keys To Establishing Your Legacy

Wisdom Is The Principal Thing

Book B-118 / $5

The Wisdom Center

I

Where You Are Determines What Grows In You.

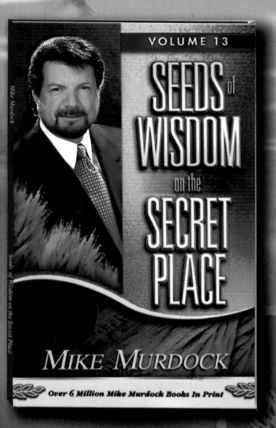

VOLUME 13

SEEDS of WISDOM on the SECRET PLACE

MIKE MURDOCK

Over 6 Million Mike Murdock Books In Print

▸ 4 Secrets The Holy Spirit Reveals In The Secret Place

▸ Master Keys In Cultivating An Effective Prayer Life

▸ The Necessary Ingredients In Creating Your Secret Place

▸ 10 Miracles That Will Happen In The Secret Place

Wisdom Is The Principal Thing

Book B-115 / $5

The Wisdom Center

Run To Win.

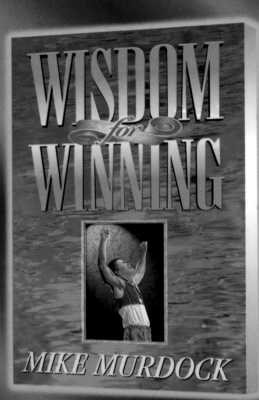

WISDOM *for* WINNING

MIKE MURDOCK

▶ 10 Ingredients For Success

▶ 10 Lies Many People Believe About Money

▶ 20 Keys For Winning At Work

▶ 20 Keys To A Better Marriage

▶ 3 Facts Every Parent Should Remember

▶ 5 Steps Out Of Depression

▶ The Greatest Wisdom Principle I Ever Learned

▶ 7 Keys To Answered Prayer

▶ God's Master Golden Key To Total Success

▶ The Key To Understanding Life

Everyone needs to feel they have achieved something with their life. When we stop producing, loneliness and laziness will choke all enthusiasm from our living. What would you like to be doing? What are you doing about it? Get started on a project in your life. Start building on your dreams. Resist those who would control and change your personal goals. Get going with this powerful teaching and reach your life goals!

Wisdom Is The Principal Thing

Book B-01 / **$10**

Six Audio Tapes TS-01 / **$30**

The Wisdom Center

THE SECRET.

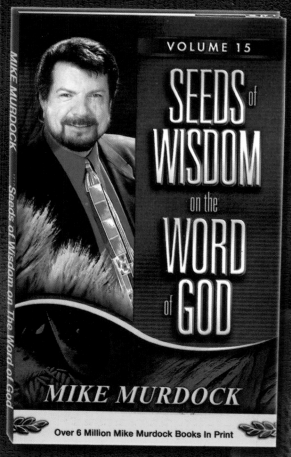

VOLUME 15

SEEDS of WISDOM on the WORD of GOD

MIKE MURDOCK

Over 6 Million Mike Murdock Books In Print

- ‣ 11 Reasons Why The Bible Is The Most Important Book On Earth
- ‣ 12 Problems The Word Of God Can Solve In Your Life
- ‣ 4 Of My Personal Bible Reading Secrets
- ‣ 4 Steps To Building A Spiritual Home
- ‣ 9 Wisdom Keys To Being Successful In Developing The Habit Of Reading The Word Of God

Wisdom Is The Principal Thing
Book B-117 / **$5**
The Wisdom Center

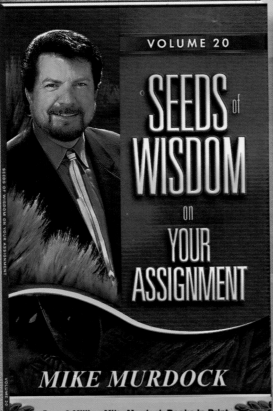

Your Assignment Is Your Discovery, Not Your Decision.

Assignment

VOLUME 20

SEEDS of WISDOM on YOUR ASSIGNMENT

MIKE MURDOCK

Over 6 Million Mike Murdock Books In Print

▶ 11 Seasons Of Preparation For Your Assignment

▶ 6 Rewards Of Pain

▶ 6 Keys For Developing An Obsession For Your Assignment

▶ 3 Wisdom Keys To Turning Your Anger Into Passion For Your Assignment

Wisdom Is The Principal Thing

Book B-122 / $5

The Wisdom Center

WISDOM COLLECTION

8

SECRETS OF THE UNCOMMON MILLIONAIRE

1. The Uncommon Millionaire Conference Vol. 1 (Six Cassettes)
2. The Uncommon Millionaire Conference Vol. 2 (Six Cassettes)
3. The Uncommon Millionaire Conference Vol. 3 (Six Cassettes)
4. The Uncommon Millionaire Conference Vol. 4 (Six Cassettes)
5. 31 Reasons People Do Not Receive Their Financial Harvest (256 Page Book)
6. Secrets of the Richest Man Who Ever Lived (178 Page Book)
7. 12 Seeds Of Wisdom Books On 12 Topics
8. The Gift Of Wisdom For Leaders Desk Calendar
9. 101 Wisdom Keys On Tape (Audio Tape)
10. In Honor Of The Holy Spirit (Music Cassette)
11. 365 Memorization Scriptures On The Word Of God (Audio Cassette)

Wisdom Is The Principal Thing

THE WISDOM COLLECTION 8
SECRETS OF THE UNCOMMON
MILLIONAIRE

WC-08 /$195

The Wisdom Center

O